TRAVELER BEHAVIOR ECONOMY

JOHN LOK

Contents

Preface

Preface

This book aims to let economic students who can learn how to use behavioral economic method to predict global airline industry passenger consumption. Also I hope any airline company management leader who can learn how to apply behavioral economic method to predict airline industry passenger consumption is better than psychological method prediction. In my book, I shall explain what factors cause the airline industry passenger behavioral consumption change as well as to give reasons to explain why applying behavioral economy method predicts airline passenger consumption behavior is better than psychological method prediction.

Prologue

How can positive or negativesocial environment influence airlines' passenger behavior

Nowaday, airline industry is entering global competition. So, any some less positive or negative social environment changing which will influence any airlines' passenger behavioral consumption change. For example, air ticket price rises or fuel price rises or the country's season is bad or the global economy is bad or the country has terrible death threat etc. different negative social environment change fastors which will influence any country passenger individual travel consumption desires.

In Special, business class airline transportation demands are also increasing, due to many business travelers need to catch planes to go to any different countries to do business as well as many cargoes need to be carried from planes to transport to different countries to sell. So, business class traveler target group behavioral consumption is difficult to influence travelling consumotion desires from external environmental factors because business class traveler target group concerns to need to catch planes to go to another country to discuss business co-operation with the country's businessmen. So, their business travel desires won't easy to be influenced more than individual entertainment travel consumer's desire.

It seems cargo and business aim of aviation transportation industry has less chance to be influenced to reduce businessmen traveler or cargo transportation numbers to compare to entertainment traveler numbers by external environment change influences, due to the business travelers and cargo transportation travelling desires is difficult to reduce travelling or transportation needs to reduce the " doing businesses to earn profit chance with another country's businessmen". However, ignorance of internal or external market dynamics, catching entertainment travelers business can be detrimental to airline profitability more than carrying cargoes or business travelers business. Because the demands of travelling different countries' travelers' consumption are still more than the demands of businessmen carrying cargoes in any countries every year. So, the global GDP of travelling income sector is still have the important position to any country nowadays.

How can positive or negative social environment change influence any airlines' air ticket prices to be risen or fallen as well as how can these social environment change influence passenger consumption desires ? For example: What is the petroleum price change influence ?In fact, the increase in petroleum price can have chance to affect every airlines passenger has a negative manner to reduce travel consumption because increased oil prices have resulted in the reduction of airline services operations, the number of airline schedules flights, even airline bankruptcies. Whether global economic inflation or deflation, terrorism threats to the country, oil shortage or oil price rising or fallening, bank interest rate increasing or decreasing etc. external factors which have the most influential causes to bring the bad or good effects to cause airline industry share price reducing or increasing or increasing or reducing air ticket price. In result, these external environmental changes will influence the global traveler numbers to be increased or decreased at the time.

To support this hypotheses, this are my research first question, such as : Does a combination of terrorism and price of petroleum significantly influence airline profit changing mostly? The alternative hypothesis was my research second question, such as: Whether a significant relationship exists between terrorism, price of petroleum and airline profitability more than other factors, such as inflation, bank interest rate or air ticket price changing of these factors to influence passenger consumption desires change. I shall indicate that the first assumption was that terrorism has a negative effect on airline profitability and another assumption was that only external factors as oil prices or terrorism affect airline profitability. Finally, the terrorism and oil shortage and oil rising price factors can influence every passenger travel consumption desire to be reduced mainly.

Terrorism attack influences traveller need

However the effects of oil price and terrorism on airline profitability was limited to a regional perspective, so oil price and terrorism external environmental change will only influence some countries' airline traveler numbers to be decreased, e.g. the terrorism attack of plane crash event to USA on 11 Sept. After the terrorism attack happened on USA 11 Sept. incident of terrorism attack was restricted to events of skyjacking, attacks on oil production, refinery and distribution. Then, due oil shortage will be caused due to reducing oil production, refinery and distribution as well as it will influence oil price is risen and airline ticket price is also risen. It will reduce travel consumption desire to some countries if their airlines' ticket prices are also increasing. Other types of terrorist activities, such as attacks on financial targets or senior government officials could have an adverse effect on the petroleum and airline industry. I think the disruption of the production or distribution of petroleum because of incidents of terrorism was costly in terms of loss of business and the inflationary effect on fuel dependent products or services.

In fact, some airlines have adopted more fuel saving technology, so whose fuel consumption would not use more than other non fuel saving technology airlines. It seems fuel price increasing will not be the only factor to influence the airline industry's traveler numbers decreasing due, the owning more fuel saving technologic airlines which air tickets prices won't influence to be risen , due to reducing oil production and shortage influences . However, due to some airlines which have fuel saving technology, so which can avoid to use more fuel to provide planes to use and which fuel costs will be reduced, then which can provide cheaper air ticket fare prices to compare the non fuel saving technology airlines. The result will cause some not owning fuel saving technological airlines which will lose travelling customers in this global airline travelling market, also the not fuel saving technological airlines need to renew their fuel technology if which want to keep their competitive abilities to avoid to close down their businesses. So, what factors will influence the not owning fuel saving technological airlines profitability to be reduce if the oil shortage factor can not influence their planes energy supply to be reduced to cause air ticket prices to be increased? To answer this question, I shall indicate another financial risk factor how it influences airline industry behavioral change.

Also, I shall indicate the financial risk of airline industry evidence from Cathay Pacific airways and China airlines against key determinants of which include interest rate, exchange rate and fuel price risk for the period of January 1996 year to December 2011 year. During this period, these key external factors which were the most serious influence to cause these two airlines choose to change their strategic behaviors. Due to any these financial risks is difficult to predict and it was also changing often, these factors will also affect any airlines stock returns which arise from changing economic conditions, e.g. fuel price movements and fluctuations in exchange rates. These external unpredicted changing factors will attribute to the air tickets cyclical demand, capital investment, fixed costs of labor and landing rights to this global airline industry. Finally, it will cause some airlines need to rise air ticket prices to reduce expenditures increasing.

However, the relationship between fuel price and stock prices varies across economies which will influence travel passenger consumption of desires. For example, the effects of oil price changes in sub-sector indices, such as wood, paper and printing, insurance and electricity. In the past, on global stock exchange market was positively significant in 2011 year. Otherwise, with respect to the U.S.A. aviation industry, some economists suggested that global airlines stock returns were negatively to percentage change in fuel prices related to any airline firm value, e.g. Qantas and Air New Zealand were negatively share price growth to fuel price risk in the short term in the 2011 year. Thus, due to these two airlines share price went down, it will influence investors who loss confidence to buy their shares as well as it will influence travelling passengers who choose to buy other airlines' air tickets to go to travel because they will feel these two airlines have business challenges, e.g. bad service quality and food quality and uncomfortable airline seat environment and poor management style. etc different bad feeling. So, these two airlines' share prices went down, it will influence every travel passenger's confidence to choose to buy their air tickets to sit their planes to go to travel.

CHAPTER TWO

Airlines fuel manufacturing supply strategy

However, there are some airlines which are the characteristic of self organization . It means that they are present in that both of oil fuel production and providing flights service in airline industry. So, these self organization airlines can control the oil fuel price by themselves. However, any self supply airline organization is also evident in efforts by businesses acts of terrorism against economic targets by adopting proactive steps, such as airline and airport security. So, it seems any self suply airline organization can reduce the risk to avoid oil price raising and terrorism attacks in airline industry risk management sector because oil shortage won't influence their air ticket prices need to be raised. Beside, these self supply airline organizations which have high technology of fuel efficient aircrafts, the use of one aircraft model, the adoption of direct routes versus customer loyalty programs and other operational cost reductions are strategies for increased profitability.

To solve oil price, terrorism etc. external risk to airline industry. Instead of high technology of fuel efficient aircrafts and self supply airline organization methods can solve terrorism attacks and oil price rising risks. However, I believe that there are other risks will threaten to airline industry. This risks concern traveller individual psychological factors influence, so it means that any airlines can apply psychological methods to predict which airline passengers' travel consumption desires. The risks include such as (1) user factor, such as : the travel country culture and tradition difference will influence the traveler chooses to prefer to go to the country to travel , the traveler's education level is high , who will choose to go to developed countries to travel, e.g. USA, UK. Otherwise, if the traveler's education level is low, who will choose to go to developing countries to travel, e.g. China, India etc. (2) economic factor, such as air tickets and airline fuel costs, (3) human resources and macro economic factor, such as political stability, economic development, educational policy, health policy, environmental policy. However, these risks occurrences are resulting in the relationship of cause and effect events. These events are not directly observable.

Such as, the complexity of relationship between terrorism and airline profitability. Hence, if global airline industry can predict when those risks occur to do protective strategic behavior. It is possible that which can understand why these risk events will occur and their protective strategic behaviors also influence their outcomes to be positive to avoid any external risk threats on the long term. However, I think hierarchy, self supply airline organization efficiency methods which are as possible predictors of user preferences to avoid risk threat events to cause whose airline businesses failure occurrences in airline industry because it can reduce oil shortage factor which causes their air ticket prices need to be rised to keep their planes can have enough fuel supply.

● Why tourism and airline industries have close relationship to influence their profitability between of them.

In my study, I suppose terrorism, profitability and the price of petroleum which had properties of distinct and interrelated close relationship. Moreover, these variables (terrorism, profitability and the price of petroleum) displayed differentiation, self replication, efficiency and hierarchy which can cause risk events to airline industry. However, I also think the other internal and external threat factors of airline industry, such as inflation, bank interest rate, business model, service quality, airline fuel or plane engine technology, air ticket pricing, brand loyalty, airline strategic management, government policy and fuel hedging of these factors which can also raise the risks to threaten any airlines existence in airline industry.

There are two basic business models in airline industry. They are network (full service) and low cost (discount) carriers. The network carrier model employs diversification strategy by increased domestic destinations, serving international routes, providing diverse seating arrangements (business, economy and first class), maintaining a complex system of offering high quality service. Otherwise, low cost (discount) airlines focus on lower air fares. To keep operating costs down, discount airlines offer shorter routes and provide point-to-point destinations rather than through sophisticated flights are primarily in domestic destinations. So, discount airlines operate a common model aircraft fleet, offer a single seating arrangement and cheaper flight services offered to compare network airlines. However, these two basic business models have their unique competitive abilities to provide any airlines existence in airline industry nowadays.

In fact, natural resource of oil is decreasing in our earth. But as the same time, human demand is increasing and oil supply is decreasing, so it also causes the oil fuel price is increasing to supply to airline industry. It influences not only to airline industry, it also impacts of higher oil fuel price to tourism, such as expansion of airports are made based on expected demand increase.

Tourism has been proven to many adverse events, including terrorism, flight disruptions. Beside, the bad natural climate change influences, such as the volcanic ash cloud event occurred in April 2010 year. So, airline industry need to concern climate change because it will cause high fuel prices indirectly. For example, the event occurred the extreme increase in operating costs for airlines in 2008 year, due to unprecedented prices for aviation fuel also meant, that despite the introduction of fuel charges, so this event causes the global airline industry recorded losses seriously. Even if alternative fuels become commercially available for airlines which are still likely to be more expensive than present aviation fuel. Thus, it seems that poor tourism will influence poor travel consumption and low airline tickets sale.

Higher airfares in the future are likely to lead to reduction in travel and cause tourists to shift from more distant to closer destination. When some of the economic responses to higher oil prices are obvious assessing the overall economic impacts on tourism is difficult. However, long term changes in global oil price rises will be similar to global changes in other commodity prices, exchange rates and income. It is therefore important to consider the impact of high oil prices on tourism from a general equilibrium perspective rather than relying only on bottom partial equilibrium. However, I believe tourism and airline industries have close relationship, such as tourism and airline industries are likely to suffer in an environment of high oil prices. Given that tourism destinations receive tourists from a range of origins, it would be useful to understand of some countries are increasing oil prices than others. Such as the net oil importing countries are selling higher oil prices than oil exporting countries generally. For example, New Zealand is an oil import country to provide planes for international visitor arrivals, so its oil fuel price is usually higher to charge to NZ airlines because any NZ airlines need to pay to foreign countries to buy any oil more expensive price. So, NZ airlines usually charge higher airfares to its visitors to compare the other exporting oil countries' airlines.

In economic theory, on income effects indicate negative impacts on tourism demand, the exact effects of higher oil fuel prices for specific destinations are far from clear. However, airline industry's different market segments show different sensitivities to air ticket fares changes. On the first hand, if the visitors are long destinations generally wealthier than average and therefore potentially less affected, as energy costs would be a smaller proportion of their income compared will be those from less wealthy groups. On the second hand, oil prices don't translate into higher transport costs especially not on air routes that are highly competitive and that are maintained for strategic reasons. On the third hand, many other factors shape tourists' decision making, including emotion drivers or those related to images, fashions and perceptions.

Increasing environmental protection awareness of tourists could also be an important factor to influence tourism consumption, instead of oil fuel price raising causes air ticket fares raising factor to reduce traveler numbers. However, oil price raising reason causes also due to high use of cars, vans and domestic air transport in some countries, e.g. Hong Kong, China countries, there are many people like to buy cars to drive. So, the private driver numbers are increasing demand to cause these countries' oil fuel prices raise in the short time suddenly. It will influence HK and China air tickets prices need to be risen , due to there are many cars, vans and domestic air transport tools need to use oil to supply energy to cause oil import numbers will increase to HK and China and HK and China airlines need to pay higher price to buy oil to use. In the result, HK and China airlines air ticket prices will also need to rise and it will influence HK and China travel consumption desire.

CHAPTER THREE

Fuel raising price solve methods

● Why oil fuel raising price factor can cause risk to airline.

In long run, implications of changes to supply and demand side conditions of oil fuel energy may differ qualitatively. For example, due to investment responses of producers, consumers and governments in alternative energy sources and more energy efficient plants, vehicles are supplied in order to achieve oil fuel price can't be risen seriously.

However, I believe oil fuel rising charge will be an important factor to influence global airline ticket fares to be also increased. Firstly, on the bank interest changing factor, e.g. bank interest rate rising which only attract more bank saving. But it can not influence the bank savers who choose to reduce relax time to go to other countries travelling. Otherwise, when the bank savers can save more money to earn higher interest in banks, who will prefer to choose to use their saving to consume travelling. Due to who can earn higher interest rate after a period of saving time. So, I believe whose behavioral travelling consumption will be raised when the banks will raise interest rate, then the bank savers won't choose to save more money in banks. So it is possible that who will withdraw more money to consume to go to travelling from their bank saving. It seems bank interest rate changing won't influence bank savers' behavioral travelling consumption to be reduced. Secondly, on the exchange rate changing factor, although any country's exchange changing will cause other countries' money value to be fallen down or risen up. However, it won't influence any travelers' behavioral consumption to be reduced seriously. Although, it is possible that the traveler won't spend too much to go to shopping when who travel to the another country and arrive the country. But, it is not possible to influence the traveler decides to reduce consumption to buy any air ticket to go to travelling. Thirdly, any country inflation also can not reduce travelers' travelling consumption easily because inflation can influence consumers who choose to buy cheaper foods and clothing and reduce entertainments in their every day life. But, one country's inflation can not influence it's citizen do not spend much travelling expenditure because travelers only spend one time or two times of travelling every year usually. So, the travelling expenditure rate of any households is not too much to compare daily essential expenditure. So, it seems that bank interest rate and exchange rate changing and inflation factors won't influence any travelers' travelling consumption of decisions to be reduced easily. Otherwise, if the oil fuel price raises too much, then global airlines' cost will be raised. So, the airlines only choose to increase their air fare prices to aim to avoid loss possibly. It seems that oil fuel price has direct influence airline income.

● Methods to solve rising air fare prices demand.

I. Why will biofuels energy be demanded ?
I suggest these methods how to avoid the oil raising price factor to cause airline air fare prices to be risen to lead the risk of traveler numbers to be reduced.
The first method: Whether aviation fuel markets will have what benefits from biofuels supply to planes. I shall refer the scope includes trends in jet fuel price, airline response to fuel price, increases and volatility and environmental goals for aviation. The aviation fuel supply industry includes production, distribution and consumption of aviation fuel and it outlines players in the aviation fuel supply chain. For example, at each airport, fuel supply chain organization and fuel sourcing could differ with regard to the role of oil companies, airlines, airport owners and operators and airport service companies. However, major jet fuel purchasers are airlines, general aviation operators, corporate aviation and the military, with most of the jet fuel in global different countries demanders being used for domestic commercial and civilian flights carrying passengers, cargos or both. Commercial aviation fuel efficiency has improved dramatically over time, largely due to aircraft and engine upgrades and operational and air traffic control improvements. So, it seems that fuel supply factor can influence airline fare prices majorly.

However, jet fuel prices generally correlate with prices of crude oil and other refined petroleum products, such as diesel. So, increasing prices and the persistent price volatility of jet fuel markets import airline industry finances in any countries. However, airlines use various strategies to manage aviation fuel price certainty, including financial hedges, increased vertical integration and adjustments in aircraft utilization and size to avoid the jet fuel raising price risk. Investments in alternative aviation fuel could be a mechanism to diversity expose to the price of petroleum. It seems the use of alternative aviation fuel would serve to diversify the fuel mix to reduce the risk of jet fuel monopoly raising price threat. If a diversified fuel mix were to avoid either fuel raising price in short term or to avoid fuel raising price in long term. Potential benefits include reduced actual fuel costs from only choice of jet fuel supply increased price certainty and lessened fuel costs. This diversify could allow airlines to become more consistently profitable and to make other investments in their businesses.

So, biofuels have potential to meet aviation industry needs, possibly including managing risks of upward fuel price trends and fuel price volatility and avoid risks with greenhouse gas emissions. So, the aviation fuels market could use biofuels to reduce greenhouse gas emission and mitigate long-term upward price trends, fuel price volatility or both.

What are the challenges of high priced oil for aviation? In fact, nowadays not the resources of oil as such, but much more the insecurity of supply, due to geopolitical instability in combination with a tight oil market makes a scenario with much higher oil prices than the world is currently experiencing not unlikely. Aviation is completely dependent upon oil as its fuel source. Since no practical energy substitute is readily available for commercial aviation, a scarcity of petroleum relative to demand will present a major aviation policy. In addition, efficiency gains, due to operational measures and new aircraft medium term. In particular, it has been demonstrated that the annual reduction rate in fuel consumption traffic unit is not a constant, but is itself also falling, in contrast to past estimates.

So, a high-priced oil scenario will have severe consequences for demand, airline revenues, the competitive position of airports and eventually airline networks, strategies and fleet development. In particular, transfer demand, short-haul and leisure traffic can be expected to be heavily affected by high oil prices, due to their relative high price sensitivity. So, different countries' governments or/and airlines are valuable to research another new and potential biofuel energy to substitute oil energy to supply our planes to reduce the threat of oil monopoly supply to influence the cause of air fare raising prices. Because the elasticity is very high to travelers, when the travelers feel air fares are rising high or even low level to influence travelers who will choose not to buy the air tickets to go to travel easily.

Will the fuel (oil based inputs) risk be higher to compare other costs to cause air ticket prices to be increased?, e.g. engineering maintenance, employees salaries, general cleaning, security office expenses etc. expenditures to airlines? If the probability-weighted upside effect on firm value when a risk is resolved favorably is greater the risk than the probability-weighted downside effect if the risk is resolved badly, then expected value work not be enhanced by hedging. So, the risk will be resolved badly to any commercial airlines. Airlines are an interesting case because the direct effect of source of risk resides squarely within the no offset in revenue functions (unlike for oil producers, for example), so value effects from costs feed directly into equity value. Most directly, the risk source is fuel costs to commercial airlines. Jet fuel is of course, a mix product of crude oil, so airlines indirectly face oil price risk. There are reasons to expect that airlines' fuel costs might to convex in oil price (i.e. absent any hedging). For example, oil prices, being generally pro-cyclical in recent times, tend to be highest when airline demand is strong. Airlines are therefore apt to use more high priced fuel than low-priced fuel over time. Airlines can raise air fare benefit is limited by the elasticity of demand. Also, cost functions could be influenced from fuel cost corresponds to upturns in economic activity overall (due to demand pressures on oil related prices), so it causes that airline's capacity delivers their services given their level of fixed capital. The essence of airlines basis risk in the case of jet fuel is essentially the time profile of the refining margin between crude and jet fuel, or the time profile of the price differential between other refined distillates and jet fuel. Thus, it is far from clear that risk management with oil is sure to add value to any airlines. It seems the impact of airline energy and any countries' domestic or foreign airline passenger travel numbers which have direct close relationship.

II. Whether the relationship between terrorism and oil prices has close relationship.
Whether the relationship between terrorism and oil prices has close relationship. It needs to judge to determine if a combination of terrorism and the price of petroleum significantly predicted airline profitability and which variable whether the further period was the most significant between the terrorism occurrence and the price of petroleum influence. So, different countries' governments or airlines need to collect samples of financial records from which country's any airline commercial passengers and cargo airlines on costs of fuel and any airline profitability. Also,

gathering the terrorism data were comparison of terrorist attacks on petroleum in oil-producing nations, and incidents of high jacking aboard any country's aircraft. When any countries' airlines or governments can judge whether the impact of airline energy and terrorism risk level is high or middle or low level. Then, which can use this sample data to measure how to do positive social change to whether to increase or reduce employment in commercial aviation industry, or ought need to invest other higher commercial activity in tourist and other travel related service businesses and when is the most right time to adopt of green technologies by the civil aviation manufacturing industry after the terrorism attacks occurrence to any country. It seems that any countries' governments or airlines which ought concern that the event of when the terrorism attacks will occur and gather past sample data to predict when the next time terrorism attacks event will be occurred and the risk will be high or middle or low level to influence global airline industry development.

III. What factors will influence airline industry's price elasticity of supply and demand?

In fact, the airline industry is largely dependent on the supply of the oil industry. Otherwise, the oil industry is inelastic. However, the increase or decrease of the price of airfare is directly related to the increase or decrease of the oil's price to fuel the aircrafts because there has no any new energy which can be substituted to oil fuel to airline industry. So, it seems oil fuel producers are monopolies to control its sale price to be raised easily.

Another factor that can affect airline industry to be directly targeted by a tragedy brought about by terrorism. The past four years, from 2001 year to 2005 year, there had been at least $40 billion worth of losses in the airline industry because of the September 11 date terrorism attacks in 2000 year. There had been an expected and significant decrease in the demand for the airline industry services because of the attacks that involved planes hijacking and crashing into key locations like the World Trade Center and the Pentagon in USA. Although, terrorism attacks can bring risk to influence fuel price rising in airline industry. However, this risk occurrence to airline industry is only that after the terrorism attacks occurred. It is possible that terrorism attacks won't occur again in the future.

Otherwise, our concerning ought be the greenhouse emissions and how it affects global warming. The air quality would be better once this new regulations are adopted. However, it would affect large airlines. So, it would increase the price of airfares because of economic fees that airline companies have to cover. Air pollution can give a negative impact on the domestic or oversea owned airline companies for long term. If airlines' planes can use clean fuel to fly, e.g. biofuel, then it will bring benefits to global airlines for long term. On the positive side, the environment would be healthier as the earth's temperature would rise, and greenhouse effect would be dramatically reduced. This positive effect can come at a cost that is greater than most people perceive. So, the environment protection travellers who will reduce travelling times to avoid air pollution is caused to influence human health. It seems that airlines need to concern to apply psychological method to predict whose travelling consumption of behavior which is more suitable than behavioral economy method.

On the psychology view point on travelers, who will be more preferable to catch planes to go to different countries to travel, due to the chance of air pollution and global environmental warm issues will be reduced to low risk to influence our health if planes can use biofuel to be energy to fly in the future one day. It seems that spending expenditure to research other non polluted biofuel new energy is one solvable method to global airline industry in the future. To solve, any airlines or countries' governments or oil producers ought choose to spend more time to research new biofuel. Otherwise, the predicting when terrorism attacks event will be occurred, it is more difficult to predict the time more than researching to produce new biofuel energy method in the future.

So, I recommend that researching the new biofuel energy or other kinds of energy to substitute the oil energy and air pollution risk these two factors are the urgent behavioral economy method is used to solve this challenge which the airlines or oil producers or different countries' governments which need to concern nowadays. Because these two negative environment factors are the most influential to cause traveller individual travelling consumption desire to be fallen among of other negative environment factors.